INTRODUCTION

Butterflies and moths belong to the second largest order of insects (next to beetles) with approximately 170,000 species worldwide. All have two pairs of wings covered with overlapping layers of fine scales. They feed by uncoiling a long feeding tube (proboscis) and sucking nutrients from flowers, puddles, etc. When not in use, the tube is coiled under the head.

The two groups differ in several ways:

BUTTERFLIES
- Active by day
- Brightly colored
- Thin body
- Rests with wings held erect over its back
- Antennae are thin and thickened at the tip

MOTHS
- Active at night
- Most are dull-colored
- Stout body
- Rests with wings folded, tent-like, over its back
- Antennae are usually thicker and often feathery

All butterflies and moths have a complex life cycle consisting of four developmental stages.

1. **EGGS** – Eggs are laid singly or in clusters on vegetation or on the ground. One or more clutches of eggs may be laid each year.
2. **CATERPILLARS (LARVAE)** – These worm-like creatures hatch from eggs and feed primarily on plants (often on the host plant on which the eggs were laid). As they grow, larvae shed their skin periodically.
3. **PUPAE** – Pupae are the "cases" within which caterpillars transform into adults. The pupa of a butterfly is known as a chrysalis; those of moths are called cocoons. In cooler regions, pupae often overwinter before maturing into butterflies or moths.
4. **ADULT** – Butterflies/moths emerge from pupae to feed and breed.

ATTRACTING BUTTERFLIES TO YOUR YARD

1. **Food** – Almost all butterfly caterpillars eat plants; adult butterflies feed almost exclusively on plant nectar. Your local garden shop, library and bookstore will have information on which plants attract specific species.
2. **Water** – Soak the soil in your garden or sandy areas to create puddles. These provide a source of water and minerals.
3. **Rocks** – Put large flat rocks in sunny areas. Butterflies will gather there to spread their wings and warm up.
4. **Brush** – Small brush piles and hollow logs provide ideal places for butterflies to lay their eggs and hibernate over the winter.

Most illustrations show the upper wings of males unless otherwise noted. The measurements denote the wingspan of species. Note that wing shape differs in flight and at rest. Illustrations are not to scale.

Waterford Press publishes reference guides that introduce readers to nature observation, outdoor recreation and survival skills. Product information is featured on the website: www.waterfordpress.com

ISBN 978-1-62005-466-6

$7.95 U.S.
$9.95 CAN

Made in the USA

BUTTERFLIES & POLLINATORS

A Folding Pocket Guide to Familiar Species

BUTTERFLIES & POLLINATORS – A Folding Pocket Guide to Familiar Species

WATERFORD PRESS

SWALLOWTAILS & ALLIES

This family includes the largest butterfly species. Most are colorful and have a tail-like projection on each hindwing.

Black Swallowtail
Papilio polyxenes
To 3.5 in. (9 cm)
Note two rows of yellow spots on forewings and orange spots on hindwings.

Eastern Tiger Swallowtail
Papilio glaucus To 6 in. (15 cm)
The similar western tiger swallowtail is common west of the Rocky Mountains.

Spicebush Swallowtail
Papilio troilus
To 4.5 in. (11 cm)
Note greenish hindwings. Also called green-clouded swallowtail.

Zebra Swallowtail
Eurytides marcellus
To 3.5 in. (9 cm)
Note white-tipped "tails" and red spot near base of hindwings.

Pale Tiger Swallowtail
Papilio eurymedon
To 4 in. (10 cm)
Inhabits dry mountain areas in western North America.

Giant Swallowtail
Papilio cresphontes
To 6 in. (15 cm)
One of the largest North American butterflies.

Pipevine Swallowtail
Battus philenor
To 3.5 in. (9 cm)
Note white crescent-shaped marks on outer edge of hindwings.

Anise Swallowtail
Papilio zelicaon
To 3 in. (8 cm)
Likely the most common swallowtail west of the Rocky Mountains.

WHITES & SULPHURS

White and yellow/orange butterflies are among the first to appear in spring.

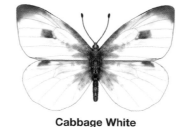

Cabbage White
Pieris rapae
To 2 in. (5 cm)
One of the most common butterflies. Larvae feed on cabbage leaves and wild mustards.

Checkered White
Pontia protodice
To 1.75 in. (4.5 cm)

Cloudless Sulphur
Phoebis sennae
To 3 in. (8 cm)
Common in open areas and fields.

Orangetip
Anthocharis spp.
To 1.5 in. (4 cm)
Common in meadows in spring and summer.

Orange Sulphur
Colias eurytheme
To 2.5 in. (6 cm)
Gold-orange butterfly has a prominent forewing spot.

Clouded Sulphur
Colias philodice
To 2 in. (5 cm)
Common in open areas and along roadsides.

Sleepy Orange
Eurema nicippe
To 2 in. (5 cm)
Underwings are yellowish. Common name reflects that it hibernates during winter.

Dogface Sulphur
Zerene spp.
To 2.5 in. (6 cm)
Note poodle-head pattern on forewings.

GOSSAMER-WINGED BUTTERFLIES

This family of small bluish or coppery butterflies often has small, hair-like tails on its hindwings. Most rest with their wings folded and underwings exposed.

Harvester
Feniseca tarquinius
To 1.25 in. (3.2 cm)
North America's only carnivorous butterfly feeds primarily on aphids.

American Copper
Lycaena phlaeas
To 1.25 in. (3.2 cm)
Common in disturbed areas and along roadsides.

Bog Copper
Lycaena epixanthe
To 1 in. (3 cm)
Note small size. Underwings are tan and black-spotted.

Bronze Copper
Hyllolycaena hyllus
To 2 in. (5 cm)
Common in wet meadows and near waterways.

Blue Copper
Lycaena heteronea
To 1.5 in. (4 cm)

Silvery Blue
Glaucopsyche lygdamus
To 1.25 in. (3.2 cm)

Underwings

Upperwings

Coral Hairstreak
Harkenclenus titus
To 1.5 in. (4 cm)
Note reddish spots along margin of hindwings. Underwings are grayish with orange spots on hindwing margin.

Gray Hairstreak
Strymon melinus
To 1.25 in. (3.2 cm)
Upperwings are brownish. Orange marks are visible from both sides.

GOSSAMER-WINGED BUTTERFLIES

Eastern Tailed Blue
Cupido comyntas
To 1 in. (3 cm)

Spring Azure
Celastrina ladon
To 1.25 in. (3.2 cm)
One of the earliest spring butterflies.

SKIPPERS

Named for their fast, bouncing flight, skippers have distinctive antennae that end in curved clubs.

Northern Cloudywing
Thorybes pylades
To 1.75 in. (4.5 cm)
Common in open areas.

Underwings

Silver-spotted Skipper
Epargyreus clarus
To 2.5 in. (6 cm)
Has a large, irregular silver patch on the underside of its hindwings. Patch is absent on the forewings.

Dreamy Duskywing
Erynnis icelus
To 1.5 in. (4 cm)
Note silvery patches on outer forewings.

Common Checkered Skipper
Pyrgus communis
To 1.25 in. (3.2 cm)

Common Branded Skipper
Hesperia comma
To 1 in. (3 cm)

Sachem
Atalopedes campestris
To 1.5 in. (4 cm)

BRUSHFOOTS

This family is named for its small forelegs that they use to "taste" food.

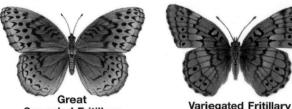

Great Spangled Fritillary
Speyeria cybele To 3 in. (8 cm)
Common in marshes and wet meadows.

Variegated Fritillary
Euptoieta claudia
To 2.5 in. (6 cm)

Eastern Comma
Polygonia comma To 2 in. (5 cm)
Has a silvery comma mark on the underside of its hindwings.

Gulf Fritillary
Agraulis vanillae
To 3 in. (8 cm)
Underwings are covered with metallic silver spots.

American Lady
Vanessa virginiensis
To 2 in. (5 cm)
Underside of hindwings feature prominent "eyespots."

Painted Lady
Vanessa cardui
To 2.5 in. (6 cm)
Tip of forewing is dark with white spots.

Milbert's Tortoiseshell
Aglais milberti To 2 in. (5 cm)

Question Mark
Polygonia interrogationis
To 2.5 in. (6 cm)
Note lilac margin on wings. Silvery mark on underwings resembles a question mark or semicolon.

Mormon Metalmark
Apodemia mormo To 1.25 in. (3.2 cm)
Has metallic marks on the underside of its wings.

Hackberry Emperor
Asterocampa celtis
To 2.5 in. (6 cm)
Is gray-brown to orange.

BRUSHFOOTS

Common Alpine
Erebia epipsodea
To 2 in. (5 cm)
Common at upper elevations.

Monarch
Danaus plexippus
To 4 in. (10 cm)
Note rows of white spots on edges of wings. Millions migrate between the US and the forests of central Mexico each year.

Red Admiral
Vanessa atalanta
To 2.5 in. (6 cm)
Note orange bars on forewings and border of hindwings.

Viceroy
Limenitis archippus
To 3 in. (8 cm)
Told from similar Monarch by its smaller size and the thin, black band on its hindwings.

White Admiral
Limenitis arthemis
To 3 in. (8 cm)
Common in upland deciduous forests.

Mourning Cloak
Nymphalis antiopa
To 3.5 in. (9 cm)

Common Wood Nymph
Cercyonis pegala
To 3 in. (8 cm)
Note 2 "eyespots" on the forewing.

Underwings

Pearly Eye
Enodia spp.
To 2 in. (5 cm)
Note 4 spots on forewings and 6 spots on hindwings.

BRUSHFOOTS

Common Ringlet
Coenonympha tullia
To 1.5 in. (4 cm)

Common Buckeye
Junonia coenia
To 2.5 in. (6 cm)
Note orange wing bars on forewings and 8 distinct "eyespots."

Pearl Crescent
Phyciodes tharos
To 1.5 in. (4 cm)
Small butterfly is common throughout North America.

Baltimore Checkerspot
Euphydryas phaeton
To 2.5 in. (6 cm)

American Snout
Libytheana carinenta
To 2 in. (5 cm)
"Snout" is formed from projecting mouth parts which enclose its coiled proboscis.

Red-spotted Purple
Limenitis arthemis astyanax
To 3.5 in. (9 cm)

MOTHS

Io Moth
Automeris io
To 3 in. (8 cm)
Note prominent "eyespot" on hindwings. Female is brownish. Male is yellowish.

Promethea Moth
Callosamia promethea
To 4 in. (10 cm)
Note white zigzag mark at tip of forewings.

MOTHS

Fall Webworm Moth
Hyphantria cunea
To 1.5 in. (4 cm)

Tent Caterpillar Moth
Malacosoma spp.
To 1.5 in. (4 cm)
Communal web nests are a common sight on trees and shrubs, especially fruit trees.

Luna Moth
Actias luna
To 4.5 in. (11 cm)

Woolly Bear Caterpillar Moth
Pyrrharctia isabella
To 2 in. (5 cm)
Also called Isabella Tiger Moth. Caterpillar is distinctive.

Five-spotted Hawk Moth
Manduca quinquemaculata
To 5.5 in. (14 cm)
Caterpillars feed on tomato, potato and tobacco plants. Caterpillar (Tomato Hornworm) has a green horn at its rear.

Rosy Maple Moth
Dryocampa rubicunda
To 2 in. (5 cm)
Maple trees are the caterpillar's main food source.

Imperial Moth
Eacles imperialis
To 6 in. (15 cm)
Told by its yellow wings and large size.

Polyphemus Moth
Antheraea polyphemus
To 6 in. (15 cm)

Cecropia Silkmoth
Hyalophora cecropia
To 6 in. (15 cm)
Note white, crescent-shaped marks on hindwings.

OTHER POLLINATORS

About 75% of the crop plants grown worldwide depend on pollinators – bees, butterflies, birds, bats and other animals – for fertilization and reproduction. Although some species of plants are pollinated by the wind and water, the vast majority (almost 90%) need the help of animals to act as pollinating agents. More than 1,000 of the world's most important foods, beverages and medicines are derived from plants that require pollination by animals.

Pollinating animals worldwide are threatened due to loss of habitat, introduced and invasive species, pesticides, diseases and parasites.

Bees, Wasps & Flies

North America is home to approximately 4,000 species of bees. Of these, the most important crop pollinators are wild native bees and managed colonies of European honey bees. Other important flying insects include bumble bees, mason bees, carpenter bees, wasps and numerous flies. With honey bee populations in huge decline due to certain illnesses and habitat loss, this can have a huge impact on food production in North America.

HONEY BEE ANATOMY

Beetles

The living jewels of the bug world, beetles are the dominant life group on the earth with about 400,000 species found in all habitats except the polar regions and the oceans. They are invaluable to ecosystems as both pollinators and scavengers, feeding on dead animals and fallen trees to recycle nutrients back into the soil. Some, however, are serious pests and cause great harm to living plants (trees, crops). Learn to recognize the good from the bad and involve your local land management and pest control resources to mitigate the spread of harmful beetles.

BEETLE ANATOMY

Birds, Bats & Other Animals

More than 50 species of North American birds occasionally feed on plant nectar and blossoms, but it is the primary food source for hummingbirds and orioles. Sugar water feeders are a good way to supplement the energy of nectar drinkers, but it is far better to plant flowers and shrubs that provide native sources of nutrient-rich nectar. While very common in tropical climates around the world, only three species of nectar-feeding bats are found in the southwestern U.S. They are important pollinators of desert plants including large cacti (organ pipe, saguaro), agaves and century plants. Rodents, lizards and small mammals like mice also pollinate plants when feeding on their nectar and flower heads.

Ruby-throated Hummingbird

Long-nosed Bat

ATTRACTING BEES & OTHER POLLINATORS

- Recognize the pollinators in your area and plant gardens to support the larvae and adults of different species.
- Cultivate native pollen and nectar-producing plants that bloom at different times throughout the growing season. Ensure the species you select will thrive with the amount of sunshine and moisture at the site. Reduce/eliminate use of pesticides. If you use any type of repellent, ensure it is organic and pesticide free.
- The plants that attract birds, butterflies and moths for pollination most commonly have bright red, orange or yellow flowers with very little scent. Butterflies prefer flat-topped "cluster" flowers. Hummingbirds prefer tube or funnel-shaped flowers.
- Create areas, out of the sun, where pollinators can rest and avoid predation while foraging.
- Supply water for both drinking and bathing. Create shallow puddles for bees and butterflies.
- Create nesting boxes or brushy areas that provide protection from predation and are suitable for pollinators to raise their young.
- Learn to recognize the good and bad garden bugs.

CATERPILLARS

Pipevine Swallowtail

Tiger Swallowtail

Silver-spotted Skipper

Mourning Cloak

Monarch

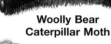

Great Spangled Fritillary

Viceroy

Question Mark

Tomato Hornworm
Note horn at rear.

Woolly Bear Caterpillar Moth

Tent Caterpillar Moth

Fall Webworm Moth

Webworm Web

Tent Caterpillar Web

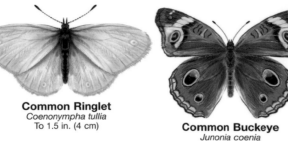